Stand Out

Se

Filip Novak

Copyright © [2023]

Title: Stand Out: Mastering the Art of Self-Promotion

Author's: Filip Novak.

All rights reserved. No part of this publication may be reproduced, stored in a retrieval system, or transmitted in any form or by any means, electronic, mechanical, photocopying, recording, or otherwise, without the prior written permission of the publisher or author, except in the case of brief quotations embodied in critical reviews and certain other non-commercial uses permitted by copyright law.

This book was printed and published by [Publisher's: Filip Novak] in [2023]

ISBN:

TABLE OF CONTENTS

Chapter 1: Understanding Personal Branding 07

The Importance of Personal Branding

Defining Your Personal Brand

Identifying Your Unique Strengths and Skills

Understanding Your Target Audience

Chapter 2: Building Your Personal Brand 15

Creating a Compelling Brand Story

Developing Your Personal Mission Statement

Crafting an Authentic Brand Image

Establishing Your Online Presence

Chapter 3: Showcasing Your Expertise 23

Leveraging Social Media for Self-Promotion

Creating Engaging and Valuable Content

Building a Strong Professional Network

Utilizing Thought Leadership Strategies

Chapter 4: Mastering Self-Promotion Techniques 31

Effective Networking and Relationship Building

Leveraging Public Speaking Opportunities

Harnessing the Power of Personal Branding Tools

Maximizing Media Exposure

Chapter 5: Overcoming Self-Promotion Challenges 39

Addressing Self-Doubt and Imposter Syndrome

Dealing with Criticism and Negative Feedback

Balancing Self-Promotion with Humility

Maintaining Authenticity in Self-Promotion Efforts

Chapter 6: Measuring and Adjusting Your Branding Strategy 47

Setting Goals and Key Performance Indicators (KPIs)

Tracking and Analyzing Your Branding Efforts

Making Adjustments for Continuous Improvement

Evaluating Return on Investment (ROI) in Self-Promotion

Chapter 7: Sustaining and Evolving Your Personal Brand   55

Building Long-Term Brand Loyalty

Staying Relevant in a Changing Landscape

Adapting to New Technologies and Trends

Continuously Reinventing and Growing Your Personal Brand

Chapter 8: Ethical Considerations in Self-Promotion   63

Transparency and Authenticity in Personal Branding

Respecting the Privacy of Others

Maintaining Integrity in Self-Promotion Efforts

Avoiding Misleading or Manipulative Tactics

Chapter 9: Overcoming Self-Promotion Obstacles   71

Managing Time and Priorities

Breaking Through Personal Barriers

Dealing with Fear of Rejection

Cultivating Resilience and Perseverance

Chapter 10: Celebrating and Leveraging Your Success 79

Recognizing Milestones and Achievements

Leveraging Success for Further Opportunities

Giving Back and Sharing Knowledge

Inspiring Others to Embrace Self-Promotion

Chapter 1: Understanding Personal Branding

The Importance of Personal Branding

In today's competitive world, personal branding has become more important than ever, especially in the realm of career development. Whether you are an aspiring professional, a seasoned executive, or even an entrepreneur, understanding the significance of personal branding can greatly impact your success. In this subchapter, we will explore why personal branding matters and how it can help you stand out in your career.

First and foremost, personal branding allows you to differentiate yourself from others in your field. It is no longer enough to simply have a good resume or impressive qualifications. Employers and clients are looking for individuals who can bring something unique to the table. Your personal brand embodies your skills, values, and strengths, showcasing what makes you special. By crafting a strong personal brand, you can position yourself as an expert in your niche and attract opportunities that align with your goals.

Furthermore, personal branding helps build trust and credibility. In an era where online presence plays a significant role in career advancement, having a consistent and authentic personal brand is crucial. Your brand should reflect your values and beliefs, illustrating your commitment to your profession. When you establish a strong personal brand, you become a trusted authority, making it easier for others to recognize your expertise and rely on your knowledge.

Additionally, personal branding fosters networking and relationship-building. People are more likely to connect with individuals who have a clear personal brand. Your brand acts as a magnet, attracting like-minded professionals who share your passions and interests. By actively promoting your personal brand, you can expand your professional network, creating opportunities for collaboration, mentorship, and career growth.

Lastly, personal branding empowers you to take control of your career. Instead of waiting for opportunities to come your way, you can proactively create them. Your personal brand serves as a powerful tool for self-promotion, allowing you to showcase your accomplishments and skills. Through strategic branding efforts, you can position yourself as an industry thought leader, opening doors to speaking engagements, media features, and other career-enhancing opportunities.

In conclusion, personal branding is no longer an option but a necessity for career development. It allows you to differentiate yourself, build trust, expand your network, and take control of your professional trajectory. By investing time and effort into crafting a compelling personal brand, you can stand out from the crowd and achieve the success you desire. So, start harnessing the power of personal branding today and unlock your full potential.

Defining Your Personal Brand

In today's competitive job market, it is becoming increasingly important to develop and maintain a strong personal brand. Your personal brand is the unique combination of skills, experiences, and qualities that set you apart from others. It is what makes you memorable and desirable to employers and colleagues. In this subchapter, we will explore the process of defining and refining your personal brand to help you stand out in your career development.

To begin, it is essential to understand that personal branding goes beyond just having a polished resume or a professional online presence. It is about knowing who you are, what you stand for, and how you want to be perceived by others. Defining your personal brand requires self-reflection and a deep understanding of your values, strengths, and passions.

Start by asking yourself some key questions: What are your unique strengths and skills? What are your core values and beliefs? What makes you different from others in your field? Take some time to reflect on your past experiences, both personal and professional, and identify the patterns and themes that emerge. This will help you uncover your true personal brand.

Next, consider your target audience. Who are the people you want to impress and influence in your career development? Understanding their needs, preferences, and expectations will help you tailor your personal brand messaging to resonate with them. Remember, your personal brand is not just about you; it is about how you can provide value to others.

Once you have a clear understanding of yourself and your audience, it's time to craft your personal brand statement. This concise and compelling statement should encapsulate who you are, what you do, and why it matters. It should be authentic, unique, and memorable.

Lastly, remember that your personal brand is not static. It evolves and grows with you. Regularly assess and refine your personal brand as you gain new skills, experiences, and insights. Stay true to your values and adjust your messaging as needed to align with your changing goals and aspirations.

In conclusion, defining your personal brand is an essential step in your career development journey. It is about understanding yourself, identifying your unique qualities, and effectively communicating your value to others. By taking the time to define and refine your personal brand, you will stand out from the crowd and create meaningful opportunities for yourself in the professional world.

Identifying Your Unique Strengths and Skills

In today's competitive job market, it's crucial to stand out from the crowd and showcase your unique strengths and skills. Whether you're just starting your career or looking to advance in your current role, understanding what sets you apart is essential for achieving success. This subchapter of "Stand Out: Mastering the Art of Self-Promotion" will guide you through the process of identifying and harnessing your distinctive capabilities, helping you excel in your career development journey.

Many individuals struggle to recognize their own strengths and skills, often underestimating their true potential. The first step in identifying your unique abilities is self-reflection. Take the time to evaluate your past experiences, both personal and professional, and identify the skills that have consistently brought you success and fulfillment. Whether it's problem-solving, leadership, creativity, or communication, everyone possesses a set of unique strengths that can contribute to their career growth.

However, it's important to remember that strengths can evolve and adapt over time. As you gain new experiences and acquire additional knowledge, your skillset will expand, enabling you to take on new challenges and opportunities. Stay open to learning and embrace the chance to develop new strengths and skills throughout your career journey.

Another effective method for identifying your unique strengths and skills is seeking feedback from others. Reach out to trusted mentors, colleagues, or friends, and ask for their honest assessment of your strengths. They may identify qualities in you that you have overlooked or undervalued. Additionally, consider taking personality assessments or skills tests that can provide valuable insights into your unique strengths and how to leverage them effectively.

Once you have identified your unique strengths and skills, it's time to focus on honing and showcasing them in your career development journey. Tailor your resume, cover letter, and LinkedIn profile to highlight these specific qualities that make you stand out from other candidates. During interviews, provide concrete examples of how you have utilized your strengths to achieve success in past roles.

Remember, identifying and leveraging your unique strengths and skills is not about bragging or self-promotion; it is about recognizing your value and confidently presenting it to others. By harnessing your distinctive capabilities, you can navigate your career path with purpose and achieve professional fulfillment.

In conclusion, identifying your unique strengths and skills is vital for career development. By engaging in self-reflection, seeking feedback, and continuously developing your abilities, you can showcase your value and stand out in a competitive job market. Embrace your individuality and confidently promote your strengths to achieve success and fulfillment in your career journey.

Understanding Your Target Audience

In the world of self-promotion, understanding your target audience is essential for carving a successful career path. Whether you're a recent graduate searching for your first job or a seasoned professional looking to make a career transition, comprehending who your audience is and what they value will be the key to standing out in today's competitive job market.

When we talk about your target audience, we're referring to the specific group of people who are most likely to be interested in what you have to offer. These individuals could be potential employers, colleagues, clients, or even mentors who can guide you towards your desired career goals. To effectively connect with them, you must first understand their needs, desires, and pain points.

To begin with, identify the industry or niche you wish to pursue in your career development. Are you interested in finance, marketing, technology, or any other field? Once you have identified your niche, research and gather information about the professionals within that industry. What are their common challenges? What skills and expertise are they looking for in potential employees or collaborators? Understanding these aspects will help you align your own skills and goals with the needs of your target audience.

Additionally, consider demographics such as age, gender, and location. These factors can influence the preferences and expectations of your target audience. For instance, if you're targeting a younger audience, you may need to focus on digital platforms and social media to reach them effectively. On the other hand, an older audience may prefer more traditional methods of communication, such as in-person networking events or industry conferences.

Once you have a clear understanding of your target audience, tailor your self-promotion efforts accordingly. Craft a compelling resume and cover letter that highlight your relevant skills and experiences, ensuring they resonate with the needs and values of your audience. Leverage your online presence by creating a professional website or LinkedIn profile that showcases your expertise and achievements. Engage with your target audience by sharing valuable content, participating in industry-related discussions, and attending networking events to establish meaningful connections.

Remember, understanding your target audience is an ongoing process. As you progress in your career, continuously evaluate and update your knowledge about your audience's changing needs and preferences. By doing so, you'll be able to adapt your self-promotion strategies to stay relevant and continue standing out in your chosen field.

In conclusion, understanding your target audience is crucial for career development. By identifying their needs, desires, and pain points, you can effectively tailor your self-promotion efforts to connect with them. Stay informed about industry trends and preferences, adapt your strategies accordingly, and consistently engage with your target audience to build a successful and fulfilling career.

Chapter 2: Building Your Personal Brand

Creating a Compelling Brand Story

In today's competitive job market, it has become more important than ever to stand out from the crowd and showcase your unique value proposition. One powerful tool to achieve this is by creating a compelling brand story. A brand story is not just about the products or services you offer; it is about the emotions, values, and experiences that your brand represents.

For every individual striving for career development, understanding the significance of a compelling brand story can be a game-changer. Your personal brand story is what sets you apart from others and helps potential employers or clients connect with you on a deeper level. It allows them to understand who you are, what you stand for, and why they should choose you over others.

To create a compelling brand story, you need to start by identifying your unique strengths, experiences, and values. What makes you different from others in your field? What are your passions and aspirations? By answering these questions, you can begin to craft a narrative that resonates with your target audience.

Next, consider the emotions you want to evoke in your audience. Do you want them to feel inspired, motivated, or reassured? Your brand story should tap into these emotions and create a sense of connection and trust. Remember, people are not just interested in what you do; they want to understand why you do it and how it can benefit them.

Another crucial aspect of creating a compelling brand story is consistency. Your story should be reflected in everything you do, from your resume and cover letter to your online presence and personal interactions. Consistency builds familiarity and reinforces your brand identity.

Lastly, be authentic. Your brand story should genuinely reflect who you are and what you believe in. Authenticity is key to building trust and long-lasting relationships with your audience.

In conclusion, creating a compelling brand story is an essential tool for career development. It helps you differentiate yourself from the competition, connect with your target audience on a deeper level, and build a strong personal brand. By identifying your unique strengths, values, and experiences, evoking the right emotions, maintaining consistency, and staying authentic, you can craft a brand story that truly stands out. So, take the time to develop your brand story and let it propel you towards success in your chosen field.

Developing Your Personal Mission Statement

In the journey of career development, one important aspect that often gets overlooked is the creation of a personal mission statement. A personal mission statement serves as a guiding compass that defines your purpose, values, and goals. It helps you stay focused, make informed decisions, and navigate through the various stages of your career with clarity and confidence.

Crafting a personal mission statement requires self-reflection and introspection. It is an opportunity to dig deep and define what truly matters to you. By understanding your core values and aligning them with your career aspirations, you can create a mission statement that serves as a roadmap to success.

To begin, take some time to reflect on your values, passions, and strengths. What are the things that energize and motivate you? What are your unique skills and talents? Consider the impact you want to make in your chosen career and the legacy you wish to leave behind. By combining these elements, you can start crafting your personal mission statement.

A well-crafted personal mission statement should be concise, yet powerful. It should clearly articulate your purpose, what you stand for, and the impact you want to have in your career. Consider the following template to help you get started:

"[Your Name]'s mission is to [action verb] [your purpose] in order to [impact]. By leveraging [your unique skills], I aim to [specific goals] and make a meaningful contribution to [industry/field]."

Remember, your personal mission statement is not set in stone. It can evolve as you grow and gain new experiences. Regularly revisit and refine it to ensure alignment with your current aspirations and values.

Once you have developed your personal mission statement, integrate it into your career planning and decision-making processes. Use it as a filter to evaluate opportunities and ensure they align with your purpose and values. Your mission statement will serve as a constant reminder of your goals and aspirations, keeping you focused and motivated on your career path.

In conclusion, developing your personal mission statement is a crucial step in career development. It provides a sense of direction, purpose, and clarity, empowering you to make intentional choices and stand out in your chosen field. Take the time to reflect on your values, passions, and strengths, and craft a mission statement that resonates with your true self. Embrace it as your guiding compass, and let it lead you to a fulfilling and successful career.

Crafting an Authentic Brand Image

In the competitive world of career development, standing out from the crowd is essential. In order to succeed, individuals need to master the art of self-promotion and create an authentic brand image that distinguishes them from others. This subchapter will guide you through the process of crafting a unique and genuine brand image that will help you excel in your career.

Authenticity is the key to creating a brand image that resonates with others. It involves being true to yourself, your values, and your goals. When you are authentic, people can see that you are genuine and trustworthy, which builds credibility and fosters meaningful connections. To start crafting your authentic brand image, take some time to reflect on who you are, what you stand for, and what makes you unique.

Once you have a clear understanding of your authentic self, it's time to relay that image to the world. This can be done through various channels, such as your resume, social media profiles, and personal website. Consistency is crucial in maintaining an authentic brand image, so ensure that your messaging and visuals align across all platforms. Use your brand image to showcase your strengths, skills, and accomplishments in a way that highlights your unique value proposition.

Another important aspect of crafting an authentic brand image is storytelling. People connect with stories, so use narrative to convey who you are and what you have to offer. Share personal anecdotes that demonstrate your journey, challenges you have overcome, and successes you have achieved. Authentic storytelling allows others to relate to you on a deeper level and creates a lasting impression.

Remember, authenticity is not about being perfect or trying to please everyone. It's about being genuine, transparent, and true to yourself. Embrace your quirks, passions, and experiences, as they make you who you are. By crafting an authentic brand image, you will attract opportunities, build a strong network, and position yourself for success in your career.

In conclusion, mastering the art of self-promotion requires the creation of an authentic brand image. This subchapter has guided you through the process of crafting a unique and genuine brand image that will set you apart in your career development journey. Embrace your authentic self, maintain consistency across platforms, and use storytelling to connect with others. By doing so, you will stand out from the crowd and leave a lasting impression on your target audience.

Establishing Your Online Presence

In today's digital age, having a strong online presence is crucial for career development. Whether you are a fresh graduate looking for your first job or a seasoned professional seeking new opportunities, building and maintaining your online presence can significantly impact your success. This subchapter will guide you through the essential steps to establish a robust online presence that will make you stand out from the crowd.

1. Define your personal brand: Before diving into the online world, it's essential to define your personal brand. Consider your values, strengths, and unique qualities that set you apart from others. Craft a clear and concise personal brand statement that reflects your professional identity.

2. Create a professional website or online portfolio: A professional website serves as your virtual business card and a central hub for your online presence. Showcase your work, accomplishments, and expertise through a well-designed and user-friendly website. Include a bio, resume, portfolio, and contact information to make it easy for potential employers or clients to find and connect with you.

3. Optimize your LinkedIn profile: LinkedIn is a powerful platform for professionals to network and showcase their skills. Complete your profile with a professional headshot, engaging summary, and detailed descriptions of your work experience and education. Request recommendations from colleagues and connect with industry influencers to expand your network.

4. Engage on social media: Social media platforms like Twitter, Facebook, and Instagram offer opportunities to connect with like-minded professionals and share valuable content. Determine which platforms are most relevant to your career goals and create a strategy for consistent and meaningful engagement. Share insights, industry news, and your personal accomplishments to establish yourself as an expert in your niche.

5. Develop a content strategy: Creating and sharing valuable content is a powerful way to establish your expertise and attract attention online. Determine what type of content you are comfortable producing, whether it's blog posts, videos, podcasts, or social media updates. Consistently create and share content that resonates with your target audience, positioning yourself as a thought leader in your field.

6. Monitor your online reputation: As you build your online presence, it's crucial to monitor your online reputation. Regularly search your name on search engines, review your social media profiles, and respond to comments and messages promptly. Address any negative feedback professionally and constructively, turning potential setbacks into opportunities for growth.

Remember, establishing your online presence is an ongoing process. Regularly update your website, engage with your network, and refine your content strategy to stay relevant and keep your online presence fresh. By investing time and effort into building your digital footprint, you will enhance your career development prospects and stand out in a competitive job market.

Chapter 3: Showcasing Your Expertise

Leveraging Social Media for Self-Promotion

In today's rapidly evolving digital landscape, social media has become an indispensable tool for self-promotion. Whether you are a recent graduate, a seasoned professional exploring new career opportunities, or simply looking to enhance your personal brand, understanding how to effectively leverage social media platforms can significantly boost your career development.

Social media provides a unique opportunity to showcase your skills, expertise, and accomplishments to a wide audience. By creating a compelling online presence, you can attract the attention of potential employers, clients, and collaborators. This subchapter will guide you through key strategies for leveraging social media to stand out and master the art of self-promotion.

First and foremost, it is crucial to select the right platforms that align with your goals and target audience. LinkedIn, for example, is a powerful platform for professional networking and showcasing your work experience. Twitter and Instagram can be valuable for building a personal brand and connecting with industry influencers. Facebook groups and online communities offer opportunities for engagement and knowledge sharing.

Once you have established your social media presence, it is essential to curate high-quality content that demonstrates your expertise and adds value to your audience. Share industry insights, thought-provoking articles, and relevant news to position yourself as a knowledgeable professional. Additionally, showcase your achievements, projects, and testimonials to build credibility and trust.

Engagement is key in leveraging social media effectively. Actively participate in discussions, comment on posts, and contribute to relevant conversations. This not only helps you establish yourself as an engaged professional but also allows you to expand your network and connect with like-minded individuals.

While self-promotion is important, it is equally crucial to strike a balance between sharing your accomplishments and showcasing your personality. Be authentic and genuine in your interactions, share personal anecdotes, and let your passion shine through. This human touch will help you create meaningful connections and stand out from the crowd.

Lastly, never underestimate the power of analytics and data. Track your social media performance, analyze engagement metrics, and make data-driven decisions to optimize your self-promotion strategy. Experiment with different types of content, posting schedules, and engagement tactics to find what works best for you.

By effectively leveraging social media for self-promotion, you can accelerate your career development and open doors to exciting opportunities. Remember, the key is to be consistent, authentic, and value-driven in your online presence. So, go ahead, embrace the digital world, and let your unique personal brand shine through the power of social media.

Creating Engaging and Valuable Content

In this digital age, the power of content cannot be underestimated. Whether you are an aspiring professional, a seasoned executive, or an entrepreneur looking to make a mark, creating engaging and valuable content is crucial for your career development. This subchapter will guide you through the process of creating content that not only captures the attention of your audience but also provides them with real value.

The first step in creating engaging and valuable content is understanding your target audience. Every piece of content you create should be tailored to their specific needs, interests, and pain points. Take the time to research and understand what your audience is looking for. This will help you to create content that resonates with them on a deeper level.

Once you have a clear understanding of your audience, it's time to brainstorm ideas for your content. Think about what unique insights or perspectives you can bring to the table. What expertise or experiences do you have that can add value to your audience's lives? Consider creating a content calendar to stay organized and ensure a consistent flow of valuable information.

When creating your content, focus on delivering it in a way that is engaging and easy to consume. Use a mix of text, visuals, and multimedia to make your content visually appealing and interactive. Break down complex ideas into bite-sized pieces and use storytelling techniques to captivate your audience's attention. Remember, the goal is to keep them coming back for more.

Additionally, don't be afraid to inject your personality and voice into your content. People connect with authenticity, so let your unique perspective shine through. Share personal anecdotes, insights, and even challenges that you have faced in your own career. This will not only make your content more relatable but also establish you as an authority in your niche.

Finally, always strive to provide value with your content. Your audience should walk away with actionable takeaways, new knowledge, or a fresh perspective. Share practical tips, industry insights, or thought-provoking ideas that can help your audience achieve their goals. By consistently delivering valuable content, you will build trust, credibility, and a loyal following.

In conclusion, creating engaging and valuable content is a powerful tool for career development. By understanding your audience, brainstorming unique ideas, delivering content in an engaging way, injecting your personality, and providing real value, you can stand out from the crowd and establish yourself as a go-to resource in your niche. So, get started today and start creating content that leaves a lasting impact.

Building a Strong Professional Network

In today's competitive job market, building a strong professional network is essential for career development. Whether you are just starting out or looking to advance in your current position, having a robust network can open doors to new opportunities, provide valuable insights, and help you stand out from the crowd. In this subchapter, we will explore the importance of networking and provide practical tips on how to build and nurture professional relationships.

Networking is not just about meeting new people; it's about cultivating meaningful connections that can benefit both parties involved. Your professional network includes colleagues, mentors, industry experts, and even friends who can offer guidance, support, and referrals. It is vital to remember that networking is a two-way street – you should always be willing to offer help and support to others as well.

To start building your network, consider attending industry events, conferences, and seminars. These gatherings provide an excellent opportunity to meet professionals in your field, exchange ideas, and learn about the latest trends. Additionally, join relevant professional organizations or associations where you can connect with like-minded individuals and access valuable resources.

Networking isn't limited to in-person interactions; online platforms have revolutionized the way we connect and build relationships. Utilize social media platforms like LinkedIn, Twitter, and industry-specific forums to engage with professionals in your niche. Join online communities, participate in discussions, and share valuable insights to establish yourself as a thought leader in your field.

When networking, always remember to be authentic and genuine. People are more likely to connect with someone who is sincere and approachable. Instead of focusing solely on what others can do for you, show a genuine interest in their work and achievements. Actively listen, ask thoughtful questions, and follow up with a thank you note or email after a meeting or conversation.

Lastly, building a strong professional network requires consistent effort and maintenance. Stay in touch with your contacts regularly, offer assistance whenever possible, and celebrate their achievements. Attend networking events regularly and seek out opportunities to expand your network. Remember, networking is an ongoing process, and the relationships you cultivate can be a valuable asset throughout your career.

In conclusion, building a strong professional network is crucial for career development. By actively engaging in networking activities, both online and offline, you can gain valuable insights, open doors to new opportunities, and establish yourself as a respected professional in your industry. So, start investing in your network today and reap the benefits throughout your career journey.

Utilizing Thought Leadership Strategies

In today's competitive job market, standing out and distinguishing yourself from the crowd is crucial for career development. One effective way to achieve this is by becoming a thought leader in your field. Thought leadership is not just about sharing your knowledge; it is about positioning yourself as an authority and influencer, someone who others can turn to for insights and guidance. By adopting thought leadership strategies, you can elevate your professional profile and establish yourself as a go-to expert in your niche.

The first step towards thought leadership is developing a deep understanding of your industry. Stay updated with the latest trends, emerging technologies, and relevant research. This knowledge will enable you to provide valuable insights and solutions to complex problems. Sharing your expertise through various channels, such as blogging, speaking at conferences, or contributing to industry publications, will help you build credibility and gain visibility within your field.

Another important aspect of thought leadership is cultivating a strong personal brand. Identify your unique strengths, passions, and values, and align them with your professional goals. This will help you build a distinct and authentic brand that resonates with your target audience. Leverage social media platforms to showcase your expertise, engage with others in your industry, and share valuable content. Consistency is key; regularly post insightful articles, videos, or podcasts that provide value to your audience.

Collaboration is also a vital component of thought leadership. Connect with other thought leaders, both within your niche and related industries. By engaging in meaningful conversations and sharing knowledge, you can expand your network and tap into new opportunities. Collaborative projects, such as co-authoring articles, hosting webinars, or organizing industry events, can further enhance your thought leadership status and broaden your reach.

Additionally, embracing a growth mindset is essential for thought leadership. Continuously seek opportunities to learn and evolve. Attend workshops, enroll in online courses, or join professional associations to expand your knowledge base and stay ahead of the curve. Be open to feedback and constructive criticism, as it can help you refine your ideas and improve your thought leadership approach.

In conclusion, thought leadership is a powerful strategy for career development. By positioning yourself as an authority in your field, building a strong personal brand, collaborating with other thought leaders, and embracing continuous learning, you can stand out and master the art of self-promotion. Embrace these strategies, and you will be well on your way to becoming a recognized thought leader in your niche, opening doors to new opportunities and propelling your career forward.

Chapter 4: Mastering Self-Promotion Techniques

Effective Networking and Relationship Building

In today's highly competitive world, it is no longer enough to simply excel at your job or have a stellar resume. To truly stand out in your career development, you must also possess exceptional networking and relationship-building skills. Regardless of your industry or profession, building and maintaining strong connections is crucial for success.

Networking is often misunderstood as a mere exchange of business cards or attending events to collect contacts. However, effective networking goes beyond that. It is about creating authentic relationships based on trust, mutual respect, and genuine interest in others. It is about building a network of allies who can support and advocate for you throughout your career.

One of the first steps in effective networking is to identify your goals and target audience. What kind of connections do you need to advance in your career? Once you have a clear understanding of your objectives, you can start reaching out to individuals who can help you achieve them. This can be done through attending industry conferences, joining professional organizations, or even utilizing social media platforms like LinkedIn.

However, networking is not a one-way street. It is equally important to offer value and support to your connections. This can be done by sharing industry insights, providing resources, or simply being a good listener. By demonstrating your willingness to contribute to others' success, you will strengthen your relationships and build a reputation as a reliable and helpful professional.

Relationship building is an ongoing process that requires patience and consistent effort. It is important to stay in touch with your connections, even if you do not need immediate assistance. Regularly reach out to colleagues, mentors, and potential collaborators to maintain a strong network. Remember to express gratitude and show appreciation for their support.

In addition to building relationships, effective networking also involves actively seeking opportunities to expand your professional circle. Attend industry events, conferences, and workshops to meet new people and broaden your horizons. Be open to collaborating with individuals from diverse backgrounds and industries, as they can offer fresh perspectives and new opportunities.

In conclusion, effective networking and relationship building are essential skills for career development. By investing time and effort into building meaningful connections, you can create a network of support that will propel your success. Remember, networking is not just about what others can do for you, but also about what you can contribute to the professional community. So, step out of your comfort zone, foster genuine connections, and watch your career soar to new heights.

Leveraging Public Speaking Opportunities

In today's competitive job market, it is essential to stand out from the crowd and showcase your skills and expertise. One powerful way to do this is by leveraging public speaking opportunities. Whether you are an introvert or an extrovert, public speaking can significantly impact your career development and open doors to new opportunities.

Public speaking is not just about delivering speeches; it is a skill that can be honed and mastered. When you take the stage, you have the opportunity to captivate your audience, share your knowledge, and establish yourself as an authority in your field. This can be a game-changer for your career, helping you gain recognition and build a solid professional reputation.

First and foremost, start by identifying relevant speaking opportunities. Look for conferences, industry events, and professional associations that align with your niche. These platforms provide a great opportunity to network with like-minded individuals, connect with industry leaders, and enhance your visibility within your field. Additionally, consider organizing your own speaking engagements, such as workshops or webinars, to showcase your expertise and attract potential clients or employers.

When preparing for a speaking engagement, it is crucial to invest time in crafting a compelling presentation. Begin by narrowing down your topic to ensure it is focused and relevant to your audience. Research extensively and gather relevant data, anecdotes, and case studies to support your key points. Use visual aids, such as PowerPoint slides, to enhance your presentation and engage your audience effectively.

While delivering your speech, remember to be confident and authentic. Maintain eye contact with your audience, use gestures to emphasize key points, and speak clearly and audibly. Practice your speech multiple times to build confidence and ensure smooth delivery. Additionally, be open to questions and feedback, as this will help you build rapport with your audience and demonstrate your expertise further.

After each speaking opportunity, don't forget to follow up with attendees and collect their contact information. This will allow you to continue networking and nurturing potential professional relationships. Consider sharing your presentation slides or additional resources to add value to your audience's experience and keep yourself top of mind.

In conclusion, public speaking can be a powerful tool for career development. Embrace these opportunities to showcase your expertise, build your professional network, and establish yourself as a thought leader in your field. With consistent effort and practice, you can become a sought-after speaker, opening doors to new and exciting career prospects.

Harnessing the Power of Personal Branding Tools

In today's competitive job market, it is essential to stand out and differentiate yourself from the crowd. Personal branding has emerged as a powerful tool in career development, enabling individuals to showcase their unique strengths, skills, and experiences. This subchapter will delve into the various personal branding tools available to everyone, regardless of their industry or background.

One of the most effective personal branding tools is social media. Platforms like LinkedIn, Twitter, and Instagram provide an opportunity to build an online presence and engage with professionals in your field. By creating compelling profiles and sharing valuable content, you can establish yourself as an expert and attract the attention of potential employers or clients. Additionally, networking through these platforms can lead to valuable connections and opportunities.

Another personal branding tool to leverage is a personal website or blog. This platform allows you to showcase your work, share your insights, and demonstrate your expertise in a specific niche. By regularly updating your website or blog with high-quality content, you can position yourself as a thought leader and gain credibility within your industry. Furthermore, including testimonials and case studies on your website can provide social proof and build trust with potential clients or employers.

Public speaking engagements and attending industry conferences are also powerful personal branding tools. Speaking at conferences or hosting webinars allows you to share your knowledge and expertise with a larger audience. This positions you as a leader in your field and helps establish your personal brand. Additionally, attending conferences provides an opportunity to network with industry professionals and expand your professional network.

Another important personal branding tool is publishing. Writing articles or contributing to industry publications can help establish your credibility and increase your visibility. By sharing your insights and experiences, you can position yourself as an authority in your field. Furthermore, publishing a book or e-book can enhance your personal brand and open doors to new opportunities.

In conclusion, personal branding is an essential aspect of career development in today's competitive job market. By harnessing the power of personal branding tools such as social media, personal websites, public speaking engagements, and publishing, individuals can differentiate themselves and stand out from the crowd. Whether you are a recent graduate or a seasoned professional, utilizing these tools will help you master the art of self-promotion and propel your career to new heights.

Maximizing Media Exposure

In today's digital age, media exposure has become a crucial factor in career development. Whether you are an entrepreneur, artist, or professional, understanding how to leverage media platforms can significantly impact your success. This subchapter will explore various strategies and tips to help you maximize your media exposure and stand out in a crowded marketplace.

1. Crafting Your Personal Brand: Before diving into media exposure, it is essential to establish a strong personal brand. Define your unique value proposition, mission, and core values. This will serve as the foundation for all your media efforts.

2. Identifying Your Target Audience: To effectively maximize media exposure, you must identify your target audience. Understand their preferences, interests, and needs. This knowledge will allow you to tailor your content and messages to resonate with your audience.

3. Building Relationships with Media Professionals: Cultivating relationships with journalists, bloggers, podcasters, and other media professionals is crucial. Attend industry events, engage with them on social media, and offer your expertise as a resource. These relationships can lead to valuable media coverage and opportunities.

4. Utilizing Social Media Platforms: Social media platforms are powerful tools for maximizing media exposure. Create a consistent presence on platforms relevant to your niche. Share valuable content, engage with your audience, and collaborate with influencers to expand your reach.

5. Creating Compelling Content: Content is king in the media world. Develop high-quality and engaging content across various formats such as articles, videos, podcasts, and infographics. Focus on providing value, addressing your audience's pain points, and showcasing your expertise.

6. Becoming a Thought Leader: Positioning yourself as a thought leader in your industry can significantly boost your media exposure. Publish articles on reputable platforms, speak at relevant conferences, and participate in panel discussions. Consistently share your insights and expertise to establish credibility and gain media attention.

7. Engaging in Media Interviews: Actively seek media interview opportunities to increase your exposure. Reach out to journalists, pitch story ideas, and position yourself as an expert in your field. Prepare for interviews by researching the outlet, understanding the target audience, and crafting compelling key messages.

8. Leveraging Digital PR: Utilize digital PR strategies to amplify your media exposure. Write press releases, submit them to online distribution services, and pitch story ideas to journalists. Monitor media mentions and leverage any positive coverage to further enhance your visibility.

Remember, maximizing media exposure requires consistent effort and a strategic approach. Stay up-to-date with media trends, adapt your strategies accordingly, and be persistent in your pursuit of media opportunities. By effectively leveraging media platforms, you can establish yourself as a prominent figure in your industry and propel your career development to new heights.

Chapter 5: Overcoming Self-Promotion Challenges

Addressing Self-Doubt and Imposter Syndrome

In the journey of career development, one of the biggest obstacles that many individuals face is self-doubt and imposter syndrome. This subchapter aims to shed light on these common challenges and provide strategies to overcome them, allowing every reader to unleash their true potential and stand out in their chosen field.

Self-doubt is an internal battle that often leads individuals to question their abilities, doubt their achievements, and feel inadequate compared to their peers. It can be paralyzing, hindering progress and preventing individuals from taking risks or pursuing new opportunities. However, it is important to remember that self-doubt is a normal part of personal growth, and even the most successful individuals have experienced it at some point in their lives.

To address self-doubt, the first step is self-awareness. Recognize when self-doubt arises and how it manifests in your thoughts and behaviors. Once aware, challenge these negative thoughts by focusing on your strengths, accomplishments, and the positive feedback you have received. Surround yourself with a supportive network of mentors, friends, and colleagues who can offer encouragement and remind you of your worth.

Imposter syndrome, on the other hand, is a phenomenon where individuals believe they are undeserving of their accomplishments and fear being exposed as frauds. This feeling of being an imposter often arises despite evidence of competence and success. Many high-achievers experience imposter syndrome, but it should not define their career trajectory.

To overcome imposter syndrome, it is crucial to reframe your mindset. Accept that no one is perfect and that making mistakes is a normal part of the learning process. Celebrate your successes and acknowledge the hard work you put into achieving them. Embrace the idea that you are constantly growing and evolving, and that everyone has room for improvement.

Additionally, practice self-compassion. Treat yourself with kindness and understanding, just as you would treat a friend. Remember that everyone has moments of self-doubt, and it does not make you any less capable or valuable.

Finally, take action. Embrace challenges and step out of your comfort zone. Each small step towards your goals will help build confidence and diminish self-doubt. Celebrate your achievements, no matter how small, and use them as fuel to propel you forward.

By addressing self-doubt and imposter syndrome head-on, you can unlock your full potential and master the art of self-promotion. Remember, you are capable, deserving, and unique. Embrace your strengths, silence your self-doubt, and confidently step into the career you deserve.

Dealing with Criticism and Negative Feedback

In the journey of career development, one aspect that can often be challenging is dealing with criticism and negative feedback. Whether it comes from bosses, colleagues, or clients, negative feedback can be disheartening and demotivating. However, learning how to handle criticism in a constructive manner is crucial for personal growth and self-promotion. This chapter aims to provide valuable insights and strategies to help individuals navigate through such situations and emerge stronger.

Firstly, it is important to understand that criticism is not a personal attack, but rather an opportunity for improvement. By reframing our mindset, we can view criticism as a chance to learn and grow professionally. Remember, we all make mistakes, and criticism allows us to identify areas where we can further develop our skills.

When receiving criticism, it is essential to remain calm and composed. Emotions can cloud our judgment and hinder our ability to objectively assess the feedback. Take a moment to breathe, listen attentively, and consider the perspective being shared. Avoid becoming defensive or dismissing the feedback outright, as this can hinder your professional growth and damage relationships.

Once you have absorbed the feedback, it is important to reflect on its validity. Consider the source and their expertise in the field. Not all feedback may be accurate or relevant, so it is crucial to differentiate constructive criticism from personal biases or subjective opinions. Use your judgment to determine the credibility of the feedback and its potential for enhancing your skills.

After analyzing the feedback, take proactive steps towards improvement. Develop an action plan to address the identified areas of improvement. Seek advice from mentors or colleagues who can provide guidance and support. By actively working on your weaknesses, you can demonstrate your commitment to growth and self-improvement.

Additionally, it is crucial to maintain a positive mindset throughout the process. Surround yourself with supportive individuals who believe in your potential. Focus on your strengths and achievements, reminding yourself of your capabilities. Celebrate small victories along the way, as they will motivate you to continue striving for excellence.

Lastly, remember that negative feedback is an opportunity to showcase resilience and professionalism. How you handle criticism can leave a lasting impression on others. By accepting feedback gracefully, demonstrating a willingness to learn, and showcasing personal growth, you can distinguish yourself as someone who embraces challenges and continuously strives for self-improvement.

In conclusion, learning to effectively deal with criticism and negative feedback is an essential skill in the realm of career development. By reframing our mindset, remaining calm, reflecting on the feedback, taking proactive steps towards improvement, and maintaining a positive mindset, we can transform criticism into an opportunity for personal growth and self-promotion. Embrace criticism as a chance to learn, and you will stand out in your professional journey.

Balancing Self-Promotion with Humility

In today's competitive and fast-paced world, the ability to stand out and promote oneself is crucial for career development. However, it is equally important to maintain a sense of humility. Finding the right balance between self-promotion and humility can be challenging, but it is essential for long-term success and positive relationships.

Self-promotion is the act of showcasing your skills, achievements, and unique qualities to others. It involves confidently expressing your abilities and accomplishments to create opportunities and advance in your career. While self-promotion is necessary, it should be done with humility.

Humility is often misunderstood as being meek or lacking confidence. However, true humility is about acknowledging your strengths without arrogance and treating others with respect and kindness. It is recognizing that success is a result of both individual effort and the support of others.

When it comes to self-promotion, humility plays a vital role in how you present yourself and interact with others. Here are some key principles to help you strike the right balance:

1. Authenticity: Be true to yourself and promote your accomplishments genuinely. Avoid exaggerations or false humility. People appreciate honesty and are more likely to support someone who is authentic.

2. Gratitude: Acknowledge the contributions of others in your success. Show gratitude to mentors, colleagues, and supporters who have

helped you along the way. This not only demonstrates humility but also strengthens your relationships.

3. Active Listening: Don't just focus on promoting yourself; take the time to listen to others. Show genuine interest in their achievements and perspectives. Engaging in meaningful conversations fosters mutual respect and collaboration.

4. Sharing the Spotlight: It's important to celebrate your own achievements, but remember to highlight the accomplishments of others as well. Share the spotlight by giving credit where it is due. This not only builds goodwill but also creates a positive and supportive work environment.

5. Continuous Learning: Stay humble by recognizing that there is always room for improvement. Embrace a growth mindset and seek opportunities to expand your knowledge and skills. This demonstrates your commitment to personal and professional development.

By balancing self-promotion with humility, you can build a strong personal brand while maintaining positive relationships. Remember, self-promotion is not about bragging or overshadowing others; it is about confidently showcasing your unique value while respecting and appreciating the contributions of others. Strive to be both self-assured and humble, and you will stand out in your career development journey.

Maintaining Authenticity in Self-Promotion Efforts

In today's competitive world, self-promotion has become essential for career development. It allows individuals to showcase their skills, accomplishments, and unique qualities to stand out from the crowd. However, there is a fine line between effective self-promotion and coming across as insincere or inauthentic. In this subchapter, we will explore the concept of maintaining authenticity in self-promotion efforts and how it can positively impact your career development.

Authenticity is about being true to yourself and presenting an honest image to others. When it comes to self-promotion, being authentic means highlighting your genuine strengths and accomplishments without embellishing or exaggerating them. It is about showcasing your skills and achievements in a way that feels genuine and aligns with your values and principles.

One of the first steps in maintaining authenticity is to have a clear understanding of your own values, passions, and goals. When you are self-aware, you can present yourself in a way that is consistent with your true self. This self-awareness will help you identify the unique qualities that differentiate you from others, allowing you to promote yourself with confidence and integrity.

Another important aspect of authenticity in self-promotion is to focus on building genuine connections with others. Instead of solely focusing on promoting yourself, take the time to understand the needs and interests of those around you. By showing a genuine interest in others, you can build meaningful relationships that will support your career development in the long run.

It is also crucial to remain humble and acknowledge your limitations. Authentic self-promotion does not mean being boastful or arrogant. Instead, it involves a balanced approach where you confidently showcase your strengths while acknowledging areas for growth and improvement. This level of self-awareness and humility will make you more relatable and trustworthy to others.

In conclusion, maintaining authenticity in self-promotion efforts is vital for career development. By staying true to yourself, presenting an honest image, building genuine connections, and remaining humble, you can promote yourself in a way that feels genuine and resonates with others. Remember, self-promotion is about showcasing your unique qualities and accomplishments, not about creating a false persona. Stay authentic, and you will stand out in the best possible way.

Chapter 6: Measuring and Adjusting Your Branding Strategy

Setting Goals and Key Performance Indicators (KPIs)

In the fast-paced world of today, setting goals and measuring performance is crucial for career development. Whether you are just starting out in your professional journey or looking to advance to the next level, understanding the importance of setting goals and key performance indicators (KPIs) can significantly enhance your chances of success.

Goals provide direction and purpose to our actions. Without clear goals, we may find ourselves drifting aimlessly, unsure of where we are headed. Setting goals gives us a target to aim for and helps us stay focused and motivated. It allows us to prioritize our efforts and allocate our time and resources efficiently.

To set effective goals, it is essential to follow the SMART framework. SMART stands for Specific, Measurable, Achievable, Relevant, and Time-bound. Specific goals are clear and well-defined, leaving no room for ambiguity. Measurable goals have quantifiable criteria that allow us to track progress and determine success. Achievable goals are realistic and within reach, considering our skills, resources, and circumstances. Relevant goals align with our long-term vision and values, making them meaningful and purposeful. Time-bound goals have a specific deadline, creating a sense of urgency and accountability.

Once you have set your goals, it is equally important to establish Key Performance Indicators (KPIs) to measure your progress. KPIs are specific metrics that indicate how well you are performing against your goals. They provide tangible evidence of your accomplishments and help you stay on track.

When selecting KPIs, it is crucial to choose metrics that are relevant to your goals and align with your overall career development plan. For example, if your goal is to increase your sales numbers, a relevant KPI could be the number of new clients acquired or the revenue generated. By regularly monitoring these KPIs, you can assess your performance, identify areas for improvement, and make necessary adjustments to stay on course.

In conclusion, setting goals and establishing KPIs are essential components of career development. They provide a roadmap for success and enable you to measure your progress objectively. By following the SMART framework and selecting relevant KPIs, you can stay focused, motivated, and on track towards achieving your career aspirations. Remember, setting goals and tracking your performance is not just a one-time activity but an ongoing process that requires dedication, adaptability, and continuous improvement.

Tracking and Analyzing Your Branding Efforts

Tracking and analyzing your branding efforts is an essential part of career development in today's competitive world. In order to stand out and master the art of self-promotion, it is crucial to understand how your personal brand is perceived by others and to continuously evaluate and improve your branding efforts.

One effective way to track your branding efforts is through the use of social media analytics. Platforms such as LinkedIn, Twitter, and Instagram provide valuable insights into the reach and engagement of your posts. By monitoring the number of likes, comments, and shares, you can gauge the effectiveness of your content and adjust your strategy accordingly. Additionally, tracking the growth of your followers and connections can give you a sense of your brand's visibility and impact.

Another powerful tool for tracking and analyzing your branding efforts is Google Analytics. By embedding tracking codes on your website or blog, you can gather data on website traffic, visitor demographics, and user behavior. This valuable information can help you identify which pages or posts are resonating with your audience, enabling you to focus your efforts on the most impactful areas.

In addition to tracking your branding efforts, it is important to analyze the data you collect. Look for patterns and trends in your social media engagement and website traffic. Are there certain types of content that consistently perform well? Are there specific times or days when your audience is most active? By identifying these patterns, you can optimize your content strategy to maximize your brand's visibility and impact.

Furthermore, analyzing feedback from your network and colleagues can provide valuable insights into how your personal brand is perceived. Seek opportunities for constructive feedback and listen to what others have to say about your strengths, weaknesses, and areas for improvement. This feedback can help you refine your branding efforts and ensure that your brand aligns with your career goals and aspirations.

Tracking and analyzing your branding efforts is an ongoing process. By regularly monitoring and evaluating the impact of your personal brand, you can make informed decisions and continuously improve your self-promotion strategy. Remember, a strong personal brand is a powerful tool in your career development journey, and by mastering the art of self-promotion, you can stand out from the crowd and achieve your professional goals.

Making Adjustments for Continuous Improvement

In the quest for a successful career, it is crucial to recognize that growth and development are ongoing processes. The ability to make adjustments and continuously improve is key to standing out in today's competitive job market. This subchapter will explore the importance of making adjustments for continuous improvement and provide practical strategies to enhance your career development journey.

One of the fundamental elements of continuous improvement is self-awareness. Take the time to reflect on your strengths, weaknesses, and areas for growth. This introspection will help you identify the necessary adjustments needed to enhance your professional skills and performance. Seek feedback from colleagues, mentors, or supervisors to gain valuable insights into areas that may require improvement.

Once you have identified areas for improvement, it is essential to set clear goals. Establish both short-term and long-term objectives that align with your career aspirations. These goals will serve as a roadmap for making necessary adjustments and measuring your progress. Remember to make your goals SMART – specific, measurable, achievable, relevant, and time-bound.

Continuous improvement also involves embracing new opportunities and challenges. Be open to learning experiences that push you outside your comfort zone. Seek out additional training, certifications, or workshops that can enhance your skill set and broaden your knowledge. Embracing lifelong learning will not only help you stay relevant in your field but also demonstrate your commitment to personal growth.

In addition to personal development, it is essential to stay up to date with industry trends and advancements. Keep a finger on the pulse of your niche by reading industry publications, attending conferences, or joining professional associations. By staying informed, you can identify emerging opportunities and adapt your skills accordingly.

Lastly, surround yourself with a network of like-minded individuals who can support and inspire you on your career development journey. Seek out mentors who can provide guidance and advice based on their own experiences. Engage in networking events or online communities to connect with professionals in your field. Building these relationships can provide valuable insights, open doors to new opportunities, and provide a strong support system.

In conclusion, making adjustments for continuous improvement is a vital component of career development. By fostering self-awareness, setting clear goals, embracing new opportunities, staying informed, and building a supportive network, you can enhance your professional skills and stand out in your chosen field. Remember, the journey towards continuous improvement is ongoing, and embracing it will set you apart from the competition.

Evaluating Return on Investment (ROI) in Self-Promotion

In today's competitive professional landscape, self-promotion has become a crucial skill for career development. While many individuals understand the importance of showcasing their talents and achievements, few truly grasp the concept of evaluating the return on investment (ROI) in self-promotion. This subchapter aims to provide valuable insights and strategies for everyone looking to maximize their efforts and ensure that their self-promotion efforts yield measurable results.

First and foremost, it is essential to understand what ROI means in the context of self-promotion. ROI refers to the tangible benefits or outcomes that result from the time, energy, and resources invested in self-promotion activities. These benefits can come in various forms, such as career advancement, increased visibility, networking opportunities, or even financial gains. By evaluating the ROI, individuals can gauge the effectiveness of their self-promotion efforts and make informed decisions regarding where to focus their energy and resources.

To evaluate ROI in self-promotion, it is crucial to set clear and measurable goals. These goals should align with your career aspirations and the specific niche you are targeting. For example, if you are aiming to secure a promotion within your organization, your self-promotion efforts may focus on showcasing your leadership skills, industry expertise, and accomplishments relevant to the desired role. By defining your goals and desired outcomes, you can better assess whether your self-promotion activities are contributing to your overall success.

Another vital aspect of evaluating ROI in self-promotion is tracking and analyzing your efforts. This involves keeping a record of the various self-promotion activities you engage in, such as attending networking events, speaking engagements, or publishing articles. Additionally, it is essential to track the outcomes of these activities, such as the number of new connections made, the visibility gained, or the opportunities that arise as a result. By analyzing the data, you can identify which strategies are most effective and adjust your approach accordingly.

Furthermore, it is crucial to consider the cost-benefit ratio of your self-promotion activities. While self-promotion is an investment in your career, it is essential to ensure that the benefits outweigh the costs. This means evaluating the time, money, and effort expended in relation to the outcomes achieved. By prioritizing activities with a higher potential for ROI and eliminating those that yield minimal results, you can optimize your self-promotion efforts effectively.

In conclusion, evaluating ROI in self-promotion is vital for career development. By setting clear goals, tracking and analyzing efforts, and considering the cost-benefit ratio, individuals can make informed decisions to maximize the return on their self-promotion investments. Remember, self-promotion is not about boasting or seeking attention but rather a strategic approach to highlight your skills, accomplishments, and value to potential employers or clients.

Chapter 7: Sustaining and Evolving Your Personal Brand

Building Long-Term Brand Loyalty

In today's highly competitive job market, building a strong personal brand is essential for career development. A personal brand not only sets you apart from the crowd but also helps you cultivate long-term brand loyalty. In this subchapter, we will explore the strategies and techniques to establish and maintain a lasting connection with your audience, enabling you to stand out and master the art of self-promotion.

First and foremost, it is crucial to understand your target audience. Whether you are an employee, entrepreneur, or freelancer, identifying your niche market and understanding their needs and preferences is vital. By tailoring your personal brand to resonate with their values and aspirations, you can establish a deep emotional connection that leads to loyalty.

Consistency is key when it comes to building brand loyalty. Consistently delivering high-quality work, exceptional customer service, and consistent messaging across all platforms will help you establish trust and credibility. People want to associate themselves with brands that consistently meet or exceed their expectations. By consistently providing value and delivering on your promises, you will build a solid foundation of loyalty.

Another effective strategy for building long-term brand loyalty is engagement. Actively engaging with your audience through social media, networking events, and online communities allows you to foster meaningful relationships. Responding to comments, addressing concerns, and actively participating in relevant discussions not only builds trust but also creates a sense of community around your personal brand. When people feel heard and valued, they are more likely to remain loyal to your brand.

Additionally, offering unique and valuable experiences can greatly contribute to brand loyalty. Whether it's providing personalized recommendations, exclusive content, or hosting events, going the extra mile to provide exceptional experiences will leave a lasting impression on your audience. By consistently surpassing their expectations, you can create a loyal following that not only supports your career development but also becomes your brand ambassadors.

Lastly, continuously evolving and adapting your personal brand is essential for long-term success. The business landscape is constantly changing, and your personal brand should reflect those changes. Stay updated with industry trends, embrace new technologies, and continuously learn and grow. By staying relevant and meeting the ever-changing needs of your audience, you can ensure that your brand remains a trusted and influential force in your niche.

In conclusion, building long-term brand loyalty is essential for career development. By understanding your audience, delivering consistent value, actively engaging, offering unique experiences, and continuously evolving, you can establish a personal brand that stands out and fosters long-term loyalty. Remember, building a strong personal brand is not just about self-promotion; it's about creating meaningful connections and providing value to your audience.

Staying Relevant in a Changing Landscape

In today's rapidly evolving world, staying relevant is crucial for career development. The only constant in life is change, and the same holds true for the professional landscape. To thrive in this ever-shifting environment, individuals must embrace the art of adaptation, continually honing their skills and knowledge to stay ahead of the curve.

The first step in staying relevant is recognizing that change is inevitable. Industries transform, technologies advance, and consumer preferences evolve. The key is to embrace this reality rather than fear it. By acknowledging that change is an opportunity for growth, individuals can take proactive steps to remain relevant.

One of the most effective ways to stay relevant is to invest in continuous learning. Acquiring new skills and updating existing ones is essential for career development. Whether through formal education, online courses, or workshops, acquiring new knowledge helps professionals adapt to emerging trends and technologies. Engaging in lifelong learning not only enhances one's skillset but also demonstrates a commitment to personal growth, making individuals more attractive to employers and clients.

Additionally, staying relevant requires a willingness to embrace new technologies. The digital age has revolutionized industries, and those who resist technological advancements risk becoming obsolete. Embracing digital tools and platforms can enhance productivity, streamline processes, and open doors to new opportunities. Whether it's learning how to effectively use social media for self-promotion or mastering the latest software relevant to your field, technology proficiency is vital for career development in the modern era.

Networking is another critical aspect of staying relevant. Building and maintaining a professional network allows individuals to stay informed about industry trends, job opportunities, and potential collaborations. Attending conferences, industry events, and joining professional organizations can provide valuable insights, foster connections, and keep professionals in touch with the pulse of their industry.

Lastly, staying relevant requires adaptability and a growth mindset. The ability to embrace change, take on new challenges, and step out of one's comfort zone is essential. By remaining open to new ideas and approaches, individuals can continuously evolve and adapt to the changing landscape.

In conclusion, staying relevant in a changing landscape is essential for career development. By embracing change, investing in continuous learning, adopting new technologies, networking, and cultivating an adaptable mindset, individuals can position themselves as valuable assets in any industry. Embracing the art of staying relevant not only ensures professional growth but also opens doors to new opportunities and success in the ever-evolving world we live in.

Adapting to New Technologies and Trends

In today's rapidly changing world, keeping up with new technologies and trends has become more crucial than ever, especially when it comes to career development. The ability to adapt and embrace these advancements can significantly impact your professional success. In this subchapter, we will explore the importance of staying updated, the benefits of embracing new technologies and trends, and provide practical tips to help you navigate this ever-evolving landscape.

As technology continues to evolve at an exponential rate, it has become an integral part of every industry. Regardless of your field, staying current with the latest technological advancements is essential. Embracing new technologies can enhance your productivity, efficiency, and competitiveness. It allows you to streamline your work processes, automate repetitive tasks, and stay ahead of the curve. By adapting to new technologies, you demonstrate your ability to learn and grow, making you a valuable asset to any organization.

Similarly, staying updated with current trends is equally important. Trends shape industries, consumer behavior, and market demands. By understanding and incorporating these trends into your work, you can position yourself as an innovative and forward-thinking professional. Whether it's social media marketing, data analytics, or artificial intelligence, being knowledgeable about these trends can open up new opportunities and give you a competitive edge in your career.

To successfully adapt to new technologies and trends, it is crucial to develop a mindset of continuous learning. Embrace a growth mindset that encourages you to seek out new knowledge and skills. Stay curious, explore new tools and platforms, and be open to expanding your skillset. Engage in professional development opportunities such as online courses, webinars, or workshops to stay updated with the latest advancements in your field.

Networking is another vital aspect of adapting to new technologies and trends. Connect with professionals in your industry, attend conferences or industry events, and join relevant online communities. Networking allows you to gain insights, exchange ideas, and stay informed about the latest trends and technologies. Collaborating with others can lead to new opportunities, partnerships, and further learning.

Remember, adapting to new technologies and trends is not just about staying relevant; it is about embracing change and embracing growth. By continuously updating your knowledge and skills, you position yourself as a proactive and valuable professional in today's fast-paced world. So, embrace the new, explore the possibilities, and stand out in your career by mastering the art of adapting to new technologies and trends.

Continuously Reinventing and Growing Your Personal Brand

In today's competitive job market, it is essential to have a strong personal brand that sets you apart from the crowd. Your personal brand is a reflection of who you are, what you stand for, and the unique value you bring to the table. To achieve long-term success in your career development, it is crucial to continuously reinvent and grow your personal brand.

First and foremost, it is important to understand that personal branding is not a one-time task. It is an ongoing process that requires consistent effort and attention. As you progress in your career, your skills, interests, and goals may evolve, and so should your personal brand. Take the time to regularly reassess your brand and make adjustments as necessary.

One way to reinvent and grow your personal brand is by staying relevant in your industry or niche. Keep up with the latest trends, technologies, and developments that are shaping your field. Attend conferences, workshops, and seminars, and engage in continuous learning. By staying informed and knowledgeable, you position yourself as an expert and valuable resource, which enhances your personal brand.

Another aspect of reinventing and growing your personal brand is to seek out new opportunities for growth and development. Look for ways to expand your skill set, take on challenging projects, and volunteer for leadership roles. Embracing new experiences not only helps you gain valuable expertise but also demonstrates your willingness to take risks and adapt to change – qualities highly sought after by employers.

Networking is another crucial component of building and growing your personal brand. Attend industry events, join professional organizations, and connect with like-minded individuals in your field. Collaborate on projects and engage in meaningful conversations that showcase your expertise and help you build a strong network of contacts. Remember, your personal brand is not only about how you present yourself, but also about the relationships you cultivate.

Lastly, embrace feedback and make it a habit to seek constructive criticism. Actively seek out mentors or trusted colleagues who can provide valuable insights into your personal brand. By welcoming feedback and making necessary adjustments, you demonstrate your commitment to personal growth and improvement.

In conclusion, continuously reinventing and growing your personal brand is essential for career development. Stay relevant, seek new opportunities, network, and embrace feedback. By actively managing your personal brand, you can stand out from the competition and achieve long-term success in your chosen field.

Chapter 8: Ethical Considerations in Self-Promotion

Transparency and Authenticity in Personal Branding

In today's highly competitive job market, standing out from the crowd is crucial for career development. Gone are the days when simply listing your qualifications and experience on a resume would guarantee success. Nowadays, personal branding has become a powerful tool that can make or break your professional journey.

Transparency and authenticity are two key components of effective personal branding. In this subchapter, we will delve into the importance of these qualities and how they can help you build a strong and credible personal brand.

First and foremost, transparency is about being open and honest about who you are and what you stand for. It involves showcasing your true self, without trying to project a false image or pretending to be someone you're not. People are naturally drawn to those who are genuine and trustworthy, and being transparent in your personal branding efforts will help you establish a strong connection with your audience.

Authenticity goes hand in hand with transparency. It's about staying true to your values, beliefs, and passions. When you align your personal brand with your authentic self, you create a unique and compelling narrative that sets you apart from others. Authenticity allows you to build trust and credibility, as people can sense when someone is being genuine or simply putting on a facade.

To incorporate transparency and authenticity into your personal branding strategy, start by reflecting on your values and what makes you unique. Identify your strengths, passions, and areas of expertise that you can leverage to create a compelling personal brand. Be genuine in your interactions, both online and offline, and share your journey with others. People appreciate honesty and vulnerability, and by opening up about your challenges and successes, you can inspire and connect with others on a deeper level.

In the age of social media, it's easy to fall into the trap of creating a polished and flawless image. However, remember that perfection is not relatable. Embrace your imperfections and share your failures as well as your achievements. This will humanize your personal brand and make it more relatable and authentic.

In conclusion, transparency and authenticity are essential elements of personal branding in today's competitive job market. By being transparent and authentic, you can build trust, credibility, and lasting connections with your audience. Embrace your true self, share your journey, and let your authenticity shine through. When you do so, you will stand out from the crowd and master the art of self-promotion.

Respecting the Privacy of Others

In today's digital age, where personal information is just a click away and social media has blurred the lines between public and private, respecting the privacy of others has become increasingly important. As we navigate the realm of career development, it is crucial to understand the significance of privacy and how it impacts our professional relationships and self-promotion strategies.

Respecting the privacy of others begins with recognizing that personal boundaries vary from one individual to another. While some might be comfortable sharing every aspect of their lives, others prefer to keep certain details private. It is crucial to approach each person with empathy and sensitivity, understanding that their privacy preferences may differ from our own.

When networking or engaging with colleagues, it is essential to ask permission before sharing personal information about others. Whether it is a friend's career success story or a colleague's personal struggle, respecting their privacy means giving them control over what they choose to disclose. By seeking consent, we demonstrate respect for their boundaries and foster trust within our professional relationships.

In the age of social media, it is easy to forget that not everyone wants their personal lives on display. Before posting about others, consider the potential impact on their privacy and reputation. Avoid sharing sensitive information or intimate details without explicit permission. Remember, our online presence is a reflection of our character, and respecting the privacy of others demonstrates integrity and professionalism.

Additionally, when using personal anecdotes or stories as part of our self-promotion efforts, it is crucial to be mindful of the privacy of those involved. While sharing our experiences can be valuable, it is important to respect the privacy of others who may be connected to the story. Consider using pseudonyms or altering details to ensure their privacy is protected while still conveying the intended message.

Lastly, respecting privacy extends beyond the digital realm. In face-to-face interactions, it is essential to listen actively and avoid prying into personal matters unless explicitly invited to do so. Remember, everyone has a right to their privacy, and understanding and respecting those boundaries is crucial for maintaining positive professional relationships.

In conclusion, respecting the privacy of others is an essential aspect of career development and self-promotion. By recognizing and honoring personal boundaries, seeking consent, and being mindful of the information we share, we demonstrate our professionalism, integrity, and empathy. In doing so, we foster trust, build stronger connections, and enhance our overall success in the professional world.

Maintaining Integrity in Self-Promotion Efforts

In today's competitive world, self-promotion has become an essential skill when it comes to career development. However, it is crucial to maintain integrity in your self-promotion efforts. The key is to strike a balance between showcasing your skills and achievements, while remaining genuine and authentic.

Integrity in self-promotion is about being honest, transparent, and ethical in the way you present yourself to others. It involves a conscious effort to highlight your strengths and accomplishments without exaggeration or deceit. By maintaining integrity, you not only build trust and credibility but also create lasting relationships and opportunities.

When it comes to self-promotion, the first step is to know yourself. Understand your strengths, skills, and unique value proposition. Be proud of what you bring to the table and confidently communicate it to others. However, it is important to avoid bragging or overselling yourself. Instead, focus on providing evidence and examples to support your claims.

Another aspect of maintaining integrity in self-promotion is being mindful of others. Acknowledge the contributions and achievements of your team members and colleagues. Recognize that success is often a collective effort, and giving credit where it's due demonstrates humility and respect.

Transparency is also crucial in maintaining integrity. Be honest about your limitations and areas for improvement. Admitting your mistakes and showing a willingness to learn and grow not only reflects integrity but also inspires others to do the same.

Furthermore, integrity in self-promotion extends to the platforms and channels you use to showcase your work. Avoid resorting to unethical practices such as buying followers or engaging in fake reviews. Instead, focus on building a genuine and engaged audience who appreciates your work for what it truly is.

Ultimately, maintaining integrity in self-promotion is about aligning your actions with your values and principles. It is about staying true to yourself and presenting an authentic representation of who you are and what you can offer. By doing so, you will attract the right opportunities and create a positive and lasting impact on your career.

In conclusion, self-promotion is an essential skill in career development, but it must be approached with integrity. By being honest, transparent, and ethical in your self-promotion efforts, you build trust, credibility, and lasting relationships. Remember to know yourself, recognize the achievements of others, be transparent about your limitations, and avoid unethical practices. By maintaining integrity in self-promotion, you will stand out for all the right reasons and achieve your career goals.

Avoiding Misleading or Manipulative Tactics

In today's fast-paced and competitive world, mastering the art of self-promotion is crucial for career development. However, it is equally important to do so ethically and authentically. This subchapter aims to shed light on the significance of avoiding misleading or manipulative tactics when promoting yourself and your skills.

In an era where information is readily available and opinions spread like wildfire, it can be tempting to resort to misleading tactics to gain attention or get ahead in your career. However, such strategies may provide short-term gains but can severely damage your professional reputation in the long run. Honesty and integrity should be the foundation of every self-promotion endeavor.

First and foremost, it is essential to present yourself truthfully and accurately. Exaggerating your accomplishments, skills, or experience may attract initial attention, but it will eventually be exposed, leading to distrust and disappointment. Instead, focus on highlighting your genuine strengths and unique qualities that make you stand out from the crowd. Authenticity will not only earn you respect but also build credibility among your peers and superiors.

Additionally, it is crucial to avoid manipulative tactics when promoting yourself. Manipulation involves influencing others for personal gain, often at the expense of their well-being or interests. Instead of resorting to such tactics, strive to build genuine connections and relationships based on trust and mutual benefit. Collaborate with others, share knowledge, and support your colleagues. By uplifting others, you create a positive image that attracts opportunities and enhances your career growth prospects.

Another aspect to consider is the responsible use of social media and online platforms. In today's digital age, it is effortless to create a false persona or spread misleading information. However, it is essential to remember that your online presence reflects your real-life character. Be mindful of the content you share, the language you use, and the interactions you participate in. Use social media as a tool to showcase your skills, engage in meaningful discussions, and contribute positively to your industry.

In conclusion, mastering the art of self-promotion requires a strong commitment to honesty, integrity, and authenticity. Avoiding misleading or manipulative tactics is crucial for building a reputable personal brand and achieving long-term success in your career. By presenting yourself truthfully, building genuine connections, and responsibly using online platforms, you will stand out from the crowd in a genuine and ethical manner, setting yourself up for continued growth and advancement.

Chapter 9: Overcoming Self-Promotion Obstacles

Managing Time and Priorities

Time management and prioritization are two essential skills for anyone looking to excel in their career development. In today's fast-paced world, where distractions are abundant and demands are ever-increasing, the ability to effectively manage time and prioritize tasks can make a significant difference in one's professional success. This subchapter aims to provide practical tips and strategies to help individuals take control of their time and focus on the most important priorities.

The first step in managing time and priorities is to gain a clear understanding of goals and objectives. By defining what needs to be accomplished, individuals can better allocate their time and energy towards tasks that directly contribute to their career development. Setting specific, measurable, attainable, relevant, and time-bound (SMART) goals can provide a roadmap for success and help prioritize activities accordingly.

Once goals are established, it is crucial to identify and eliminate time-wasting activities. This may involve assessing daily routines, identifying distractions, and implementing strategies to minimize their impact. Techniques such as time blocking, where specific time slots are dedicated to specific tasks, can help individuals stay focused and avoid multitasking, which often leads to reduced productivity.

Prioritization is another key aspect of effective time management. Not all tasks are created equal, and it is essential to distinguish between urgent and important tasks. Urgent tasks demand immediate attention, while important tasks contribute to long-term goals. By prioritizing important tasks over urgent but less significant ones, individuals can ensure they are making progress towards their career development objectives.

Moreover, delegation and effective communication can play a vital role in managing time and priorities. Learning to delegate tasks to capable colleagues or outsourcing non-essential activities can free up valuable time for more critical responsibilities. Additionally, clear and concise communication with supervisors, team members, and stakeholders can help set realistic expectations and avoid unnecessary time-consuming detours.

To enhance time management skills, it is also beneficial to leverage technology and tools. Utilizing productivity apps, project management software, and calendar systems can help individuals stay organized, streamline tasks, and set reminders for deadlines or important meetings.

In conclusion, mastering the art of managing time and priorities is crucial for career development. By setting clear goals, eliminating time-wasting activities, prioritizing tasks, delegating when necessary, and utilizing technology, individuals can take control of their time and maximize their productivity. These skills not only contribute to professional success but also facilitate a more balanced and fulfilling life. By implementing the strategies outlined in this subchapter, individuals can stand out in their careers and achieve their goals.

Breaking Through Personal Barriers

In today's competitive world, personal barriers can often hinder our progress and prevent us from achieving our full potential. These barriers can manifest in various forms such as self-doubt, fear of failure, lack of confidence, or even a negative mindset. However, it is essential to recognize and address these barriers in order to excel in our careers and achieve personal growth.

In this subchapter, we will explore effective strategies to break through personal barriers and unleash our true potential. Whether you are a recent graduate, a mid-career professional, or someone looking to make a career change, these techniques will help you overcome obstacles and propel your career development.

One of the first steps to breaking through personal barriers is self-awareness. Take the time to identify the barriers that are holding you back. Are you afraid of taking risks? Do you struggle with self-confidence? By pinpointing these barriers, you can begin working on strategies to overcome them.

Next, it is important to adopt a growth mindset. Understand that setbacks and failures are part of the learning process. Embrace them as opportunities for growth and learning, rather than allowing them to discourage you. Cultivating a positive and resilient mindset will enable you to bounce back from challenges and persevere in the face of adversity.

Another powerful technique is to set clear and achievable goals. Define what success means to you and establish a roadmap to reach your objectives. Break down your goals into smaller, manageable steps that you can tackle one at a time. Celebrate each milestone along the way, as these small victories will boost your motivation and confidence.

Seeking support from mentors and networking with like-minded professionals can also help you overcome personal barriers. Connect with individuals who have overcome similar obstacles and learn from their experiences. Surrounding yourself with a strong support network will provide you with valuable insights, encouragement, and accountability.

Finally, remember to practice self-care. Taking care of your physical and mental well-being is crucial for breaking through personal barriers. Prioritize activities that promote self-care, such as exercise, meditation, and pursuing hobbies that bring you joy. When you prioritize self-care, you will have the energy and mental clarity to tackle challenges head-on.

Breaking through personal barriers is a journey that requires commitment, resilience, and self-reflection. By implementing these strategies, you can overcome obstacles, unleash your true potential, and excel in your career development. Remember, you have the power to break free from self-imposed limitations and stand out in a competitive world.

Dealing with Fear of Rejection

Rejection is an inevitable part of life, and it is something that many people fear. Whether it is in our personal relationships or professional endeavors, the fear of rejection can hold us back from reaching our full potential. In the realm of career development, this fear can be particularly detrimental, as it can prevent us from taking risks, pursuing opportunities, and promoting ourselves effectively.

Understanding the fear of rejection is the first step towards overcoming it. Often, this fear stems from a deep-seated need for acceptance and validation. We all want to be liked and appreciated by others, and the thought of being rejected can be a blow to our self-esteem. However, it is important to recognize that rejection does not define our worth or abilities.

To overcome the fear of rejection, it is crucial to change our mindset. Instead of viewing rejection as a personal failure, we can reframe it as an opportunity for growth and learning. Each rejection can provide valuable feedback that can help us improve and refine our skills. By embracing rejection as a natural part of the process, we can develop resilience and bounce back stronger than ever.

Another effective strategy for dealing with the fear of rejection is to face it head-on. This means actively seeking out opportunities that may result in rejection. Whether it is applying for a challenging job, pitching a project, or asking for a promotion, putting ourselves out there can be intimidating. However, the more we expose ourselves to rejection, the more desensitized we become. With each experience, we build up our confidence and become better equipped to handle rejection in the future.

Additionally, surrounding ourselves with a supportive network can make a world of difference. Seeking advice and guidance from mentors, friends, or career coaches can provide valuable insights and encouragement. Their perspective can help us gain a more balanced view of our abilities and remind us that rejection is not a reflection of our worth.

In conclusion, the fear of rejection is a common obstacle that can hinder our career development. However, by understanding the root causes of this fear, changing our mindset, facing rejection head-on, and seeking support, we can learn to navigate rejection with grace and resilience. Remember, rejection is simply a part of the journey to success, and each rejection brings us one step closer to our goals.

Cultivating Resilience and Perseverance

In the challenging world of career development, resilience and perseverance are essential qualities that can make the difference between success and stagnation. In this subchapter, we will explore the significance of these two traits and provide practical tips on how to cultivate them to stand out and master the art of self-promotion.

Resilience is the ability to bounce back from setbacks, adapt to change, and remain focused on your goals. It is a crucial skill in today's fast-paced and unpredictable job market. Resilient individuals are not discouraged by failures or rejections; instead, they see them as opportunities for growth and learning. To cultivate resilience, it is important to develop a positive mindset, maintain a strong support network, and engage in self-care activities to recharge your emotional and physical well-being.

Perseverance, on the other hand, is the ability to stay committed to your goals and overcome obstacles along the way. It is about having the determination and tenacity to keep going, even when faced with challenges and setbacks. Perseverance requires a clear vision of your career objectives, a strong work ethic, and the ability to stay focused on your long-term goals. To cultivate perseverance, break down your goals into manageable steps, celebrate small victories along the way, and seek feedback and guidance from mentors or career coaches.

Building resilience and perseverance go hand in hand with developing a growth mindset. Embrace the idea that setbacks are not failures but opportunities for learning and improvement. Take the time to reflect on your experiences, identify areas for growth, and adjust your approach accordingly. Surround yourself with positive, supportive individuals who believe in your potential and can provide guidance and encouragement when needed.

Remember, cultivating resilience and perseverance is not an overnight process. It requires consistent effort and a commitment to personal growth. By developing these qualities, you will not only stand out in your career but also build the inner strength and confidence needed to navigate any challenges that come your way.

In conclusion, resilience and perseverance are essential traits for career development. By cultivating these qualities, you can overcome obstacles, bounce back from setbacks, and ultimately stand out in your field. Embrace the idea of personal growth, surround yourself with positive influences, and stay committed to your long-term goals. With resilience and perseverance, you can master the art of self-promotion and achieve the career success you deserve.

Chapter 10: Celebrating and Leveraging Your Success

Recognizing Milestones and Achievements

In the journey of career development, it is essential for individuals to not only focus on their goals and aspirations, but also take the time to acknowledge and celebrate their milestones and achievements along the way. Recognizing these accomplishments not only boosts motivation and self-confidence, but also serves as a reminder of the progress made and the potential for further growth.

Achievements come in various forms and sizes, from small victories in everyday tasks to major breakthroughs in professional projects. It is crucial to remember that every step forward counts, regardless of its magnitude. By recognizing and embracing these milestones, individuals can create a positive mindset that fuels their drive to excel.

One effective way to acknowledge achievements is through self-reflection. Take the time to sit down and evaluate the progress made. Consider the challenges faced, the skills developed, and the valuable lessons learned. By reflecting on these experiences, individuals can gain a better understanding of their strengths and weaknesses, enabling them to make informed decisions about their career paths.

Celebrating milestones should not be limited to personal recognition alone. Sharing achievements with others is equally important, as it not only fosters a sense of community, but also allows for networking opportunities and potential collaborations. By sharing accomplishments, individuals can inspire and motivate others, creating a supportive environment conducive to growth and success.

Furthermore, recognizing milestones and achievements can also be done through formal channels, such as performance evaluations or awards ceremonies. These acknowledgments not only provide validation for hard work, but also serve as a record of accomplishments that can be showcased in future endeavors.

In conclusion, recognizing milestones and achievements is an essential aspect of career development. By taking the time to acknowledge and celebrate these moments, individuals not only boost their self-confidence but also maintain motivation and drive. Whether through self-reflection, sharing accomplishments with others, or formal recognition, embracing these milestones creates a positive mindset that propels individuals towards further success. So, let us remember to celebrate every achievement, big or small, as we strive to stand out and master the art of self-promotion in our careers.

Leveraging Success for Further Opportunities

In the fast-paced and competitive world of career development, it is essential to not only strive for success but also to leverage that success for further opportunities. In this subchapter, we will explore the art of self-promotion and how to effectively utilize your achievements to propel your career to new heights.

One of the first steps to leveraging your success is to recognize and celebrate your accomplishments. Take the time to reflect on your achievements, whether big or small, and acknowledge the hard work and dedication that went into them. By acknowledging your successes, you not only boost your confidence but also gain a clearer understanding of your unique value proposition.

Once you have recognized your achievements, it is important to communicate them effectively. This can be done through various channels such as updating your resume, creating a personal website, or utilizing social media platforms. Craft a compelling narrative that highlights your accomplishments and demonstrates your expertise. Remember to tailor your message to your specific audience, ensuring that your self-promotion efforts align with their interests and needs.

Networking is another powerful tool for leveraging your success. Attend industry events, join professional associations, and engage in conversations with like-minded individuals. Build meaningful connections and share your success stories, as this will not only enhance your professional reputation but also open doors to new opportunities. Additionally, consider mentoring others in your field, as this further establishes your expertise and can lead to valuable connections and collaborations.

Leveraging success also involves staying up-to-date with industry trends and continuously honing your skills. Seek out learning opportunities, whether through workshops, courses, or conferences, to stay ahead of the curve and remain a valuable asset to your industry. By continuously improving and expanding your skillset, you not only increase your value as a professional but also position yourself as a leader in your niche.

In conclusion, leveraging success for further opportunities is a crucial aspect of career development. By recognizing and celebrating your achievements, effectively communicating them, networking, and staying current in your field, you can propel your career to new heights. So, stand out from the crowd, master the art of self-promotion, and seize the opportunities that come your way. Your success is just the beginning of an exciting journey towards even greater achievements.

Giving Back and Sharing Knowledge

In the ever-evolving world of career development, there is one aspect that remains constant and invaluable - giving back and sharing knowledge. The act of imparting wisdom and supporting others along their professional journey is not only a noble endeavor but also a powerful tool for personal growth and self-promotion.

No matter where you are in your career, whether you are just starting out or have reached the pinnacle of success, there is always something you can offer to others. Sharing your knowledge and experiences not only benefits those who seek guidance but also helps solidify your own expertise and reputation as an industry leader.

One of the most effective ways to give back is through mentorship. Becoming a mentor allows you to guide and inspire others, providing them with valuable insights and advice based on your own experiences. By investing your time and energy in someone else's development, you not only contribute to their success but also enhance your own leadership skills and gain a fresh perspective on your own career.

Another way to give back is by participating in professional networking events, workshops, or conferences. These platforms provide opportunities to share your knowledge, contribute to panel discussions, or deliver presentations. By actively engaging in these activities, you not only showcase your expertise to a wider audience but also establish yourself as a thought leader in your field.

Additionally, sharing knowledge can take the form of writing articles, blog posts, or even publishing a book. By putting your thoughts and insights into writing, you can reach a broader audience and make a lasting impact. This not only establishes your credibility but also opens doors to new opportunities and collaborations.

Lastly, volunteering your time and skills to non-profit organizations or educational institutions is an excellent way to give back. By offering your expertise in a pro bono capacity, you can make a meaningful difference in the lives of others while expanding your network and gaining exposure to new professional experiences.

In conclusion, giving back and sharing knowledge is a crucial aspect of career development. It not only benefits others by providing guidance and support but also contributes to your own growth and self-promotion. By becoming a mentor, participating in professional events, sharing your expertise through writing, or volunteering your skills, you can make a lasting impact in your industry while solidifying your reputation as a leader. Remember, the act of giving back is not only a selfless gesture but also a powerful tool for standing out and mastering the art of self-promotion in your career.

Inspiring Others to Embrace Self-Promotion

In today's competitive world, self-promotion has become a crucial skill for career development. However, it is not only important for individuals to master this art for their own success but also to inspire others to do the same. By encouraging others to embrace self-promotion, we can create a culture of personal growth and professional advancement.

One of the key reasons why inspiring others to embrace self-promotion is essential is because it fosters a supportive environment. When individuals are confident in promoting their skills and achievements, it creates a positive atmosphere where everyone feels encouraged to showcase their own talents. By celebrating each other's successes, we can create a collaborative and uplifting workplace that benefits everyone.

Moreover, inspiring others to embrace self-promotion helps to break down the barriers of self-doubt and imposter syndrome. Many individuals may shy away from promoting themselves due to fear of being perceived as arrogant or boastful. However, by sharing stories of personal growth and highlighting the positive outcomes of self-promotion, we can help others overcome these self-limiting beliefs. By normalizing self-promotion as a necessary tool for career development, we empower individuals to step out of their comfort zones and seize opportunities.

Furthermore, inspiring others to embrace self-promotion can have a significant impact on their overall career trajectory. By providing guidance and mentorship, we can help individuals identify their unique strengths and develop effective self-promotion strategies. This can include encouraging them to create a personal brand, guiding them in crafting compelling resumes and cover letters, or teaching them how to leverage networking and social media platforms. By sharing our own success stories and offering practical advice, we can inspire others to take charge of their professional journeys.

Ultimately, inspiring others to embrace self-promotion is not just about personal gain but about fostering a culture of continuous growth and development. By encouraging individuals to showcase their talents and amplify their achievements, we can create a ripple effect of success within our organizations and communities. So, let us lead by example, inspire others to embrace self-promotion, and collectively elevate our careers to new heights.

Printed in the USA
CPSIA information can be obtained
at www.ICGtesting.com
LVHW021317240524
780937LV00013B/833